LEEDS UNITED

Andy Croft

Published in association with The Basic Skills Agency

Hodder & Stoughton
A MEMBER OF THE HODDER HEADLINE GROUP

Acknowledgements

Cover: Alex Morton/Action Images.

Photographs: pp. 16, 18, 21, 23 © Allsport UK, London; pp. 10, 12 © Hulton Getty, London; pp. 2, 6 © Yorkshire Post Newspapers.

Orders: please contact Bookpoint Ltd, 39 Milton Park, Abingdon, Oxon OX14 4TD. Telephone: (44) 01235 400414, Fax: (44) 01235 400454. Lines are open from 9.00–6.00, Monday to Saturday, with a 24 hour message answering service. Email address: orders@bookpoint.co.uk

British Library Cataloguing in Publication Data
A catalogue record for this title is available from The British Library

ISBN 0 340 74738 2

First published 1999
Impression number   10 9 8 7 6 5 4 3 2 1
Year   2004 2003 2002 2001 2000 1999

Copyright © 1999 Andy Croft

Typeset by Fakenham Photosetting Ltd, Fakenham, Norfolk.
Printed in Great Britain for Hodder & Stoughton Educational, a division of Hodder Headline Plc, 338 Euston Road, London NW1 3BH by Redwood Books, Trowbridge, Wiltshire.

Contents

1 Beginnings

Football started late in Leeds.
People in Leeds liked rugby best.

In 1877 some soccer fans founded Hunslet AFC.
But they didn't last long.
Leeds FC came next.
But they didn't last long either.
Hunslet tried to start again.
They didn't have a ground.
So they rented a rugby pitch.
It was opposite the Peacock pub
on Elland Road.

Leeds City football team 1908–9.

Hunslet changed their name to Leeds City.
City played in blue and gold.
They started playing
in the West Yorkshire League.
3,000 people turned up
to watch their first game.
They lost 2–0 to Hull City.

Next season they were elected
to the Football League.
Their first match was at Bradford City.
There were 15,000 people
at Valley Parade that day.
Leeds lost 1–0.

Then came the First World War.
There was no professional football.
Just friendlies.
Leeds had really improved.
Leeds City were now one of the best teams
in the country.
But they paid their players.
This was against FA rules.
The FA found out.
In 1919 Leeds City were expelled
from the League.
The players were sold
to pay the club's debts.
That was the end of Leeds City.

2 United!

Huddersfield Town wanted to move
to Elland Road.
The Leeds directors thought
it was a good idea.
But the fans didn't!

The supporters formed a new club.
It was called Leeds United.
They took over Elland Road.
They put adverts for players in the local paper.
They played in the Midlands League.
In 1920 Leeds were allowed to join
the Football League.

The new Leeds United 1920–21.

United played in blue and white stripes.
16,000 people saw their first home match.
They lost again.
2–1 to South Shields.

Four seasons later
United were Second Division Champions.
But they were soon relegated.
United had some good players.
Willis Edwards.
John White.
George and Jack Milburn.
Tom Jennings played 167 games for Leeds
and scored 112 goals.
He once scored 16 goals in seven games!

But United never had much money
to buy players.
They couldn't even afford
to sew numbers on their shirts!

Leeds had one of the worst cup records
in the country.
They never even reached the quarter-finals.

They made it back to the First Division in 1932.
But in 1946–7 they slumped again.
They won only one point from 23 away games.

United were back in the Second Division.

3 Monkey Glands

In 1948 Major Frank Buckley became manager.
He was a very famous manager.
He wanted his players to be fit.
He made them dance in training.
He even gave them a secret potion
called 'Monkey Glands'.
But they couldn't get out
of the Second Division.

United had the best centre-forward
in the country.
He was also a brilliant centre-half.
His name was John Charles.
He scored 42 goals in one season.
He also scored 15 goals for Wales.

John Charles scored 42 goals for Leeds in one season and also played for Wales.

Leeds managed to reach the quarter-finals
of the FA Cup.
But they were knocked out by Arsenal.
And they couldn't get out
of the Second Division.

In 1956 the West Stand burnt down.
Leeds sold Charles to Juventus
to raise money to build a new stand.
Juventus paid £65,000.
This was twice the British record!

Leeds began to slip without John Charles.

At the start of the 1960s
they were bottom of the Second Division.

The Leeds Cup Final squad in 1965.

4 The Revie Years

In 1961 Don Revie became manager.
He had played for Leeds.
But he had never been a manager before.

Revie asked Matt Busby
how to be a good manager.
Matt Busby said,
'All you have to do
is treat your players well.
Be honest with them and never lie to them.
In return they'll do anything for you.'

This was the secret of Don Revie's success.
He built a team on loyalty.
He looked after his players.
They were like a family.
They were a hard team.
But they were skilful.
Revie made United wear an all-white kit.
Just like Real Madrid.

For ten years Leeds were the best team
in Europe.
In goal were Gary Sprake and David Harvey.
Paul Reaney, Terry Cooper, Jack Charlton
and Norman Hunter were in defence.
Paul Madeley, Billy Bremner, Trevor Cherry
and Johnny Giles were in midfield.
Allan Clarke, Mick Jones, Eddie Gray
and Peter Lorimer were in attack.

What a brilliant squad!

In 1968–9 Leeds lost only two League games
all season!
In 1969–70 they lost only three matches
out of 52!
In 1973–4 they played 29 matches
without losing!
In 12 seasons they played 87 games
in Europe!

Leeds United's Cup Record 1964–75

1964 Second Division champions
1965 FA Cup finalists
      second in the League
1966 Second in the League
1967 Fairs Cup finalists
      fourth in the League
1968 League Cup winners
      Fairs Cup winners
      fourth in the League
1969 Champions
      Charity Shield winners
1970 FA Cup finalists
      second in the League
1971 Fairs Cup finalists
      second in the League
1972 FA Cup winners
      second in the League
1973 FA Cup finalists
      European Cup Winners Cup finalists
      third in the League
1974 Champions
1975 European Cup finalists

Billy Bremner played for Leeds
in the 1970s and 1980s.

5 Second Division Again

In 1974 Revie left Leeds
to become the England manager.

Lots of managers tried to follow Don Revie.
But no one could.
Leeds had seven managers
in the next 11 years.
Brian Clough only lasted 44 days
in the job!

Eddie Gray, Billy Bremner and Allan Clarke
tried to bring the glory days back.

But nothing could stop United
slipping down the table.

In 1982 they were relegated.

They spent the rest of the 1980s
back in the Second Division.

Howard Wilkinson made Leeds League Champions again in just two years.

6 Champions Again!

In 1988 Howard Wilkinson became manager.

He took down the photos of Revie's teams.
'That's all history,' he said.
Howard Wilkinson wanted
to make history himself.
He did.
He took just two years to take Leeds
back to the top.
He built one of the strongest teams
in the country.

Eric Cantona
Rod Wallace
Carlton Palmer
David Batty
John Lukic
Garry McAllister
Gary Speed
Lee Chapman
Gordon Strachan

In 1990 United won the Second Division.
In 1992 the Championship came back to Leeds!

Leeds captain Gordon Strachan
with the Championship Cup in 1992.

7 George Graham and David O'Leary

In 1996 George Graham took over as manager.
He was already a very successful manager.
At Arsenal he won the Championship,
the FA Cup, the League Cup
and the Cup Winners Cup.

George Graham began to build
another great Leeds team.
But then he moved to Spurs.
His assistant took over at Leeds.
His name is David O'Leary.
He is one of the best-paid managers
in the Premiership.
He has not managed a club before.
But he has some brilliant players
at Leeds.

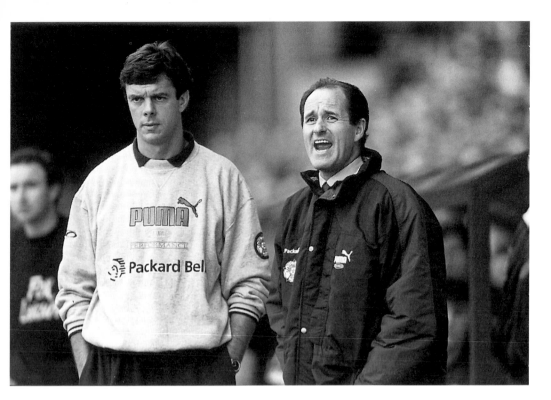

David O'Leary (left) and George Graham (right)
made Leeds great again.

Leeds fans think this team
is going to win something.
Soon.
Maybe this season.
One thing is certain.
Leeds have a team to shout about again.
Leeds have a team worth singing about.

In the words of the old Leeds song:

'Here we go with Leeds United,
We're gonna give the boys a hand,
Stand up and sing for Leeds United,
They are the greatest in the land.
Marching on together,
We're gonna see you win,
La, la, la, la, la, la,
We are so proud, we shout it loud,
We love you – Leeds, Leeds, Leeds!'

Glossary

Championship   a contest for the top place in a sport

Don Revie   (pronounced Re-vy)

Juventus   a team from Italy (pronounced you-ven-tus)

Matt Busby   manager of Manchester United, 1945–70

relegated   moved down to a lower division

If you have enjoyed reading this book, you may be interested in other titles in the *Livewire* series.

Derby County
West Ham United
Sheffield Wednesday
Blackburn Rovers
Manchester United
Arsenal
Newcastle United